Dedicated to all of those who
were ever in their own
"Pit"

**It started out as a small dent.
My dent.**

As I looked, my dent grew bigger.
Not a lot, but definitely bigger.

I saw people gathering
around to look at my dent.
I became angry.
This was my dent!

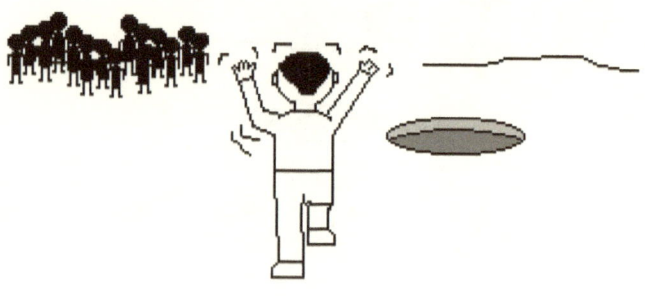

Go away!" I shouted.
One by one they left.
Some were sad.
Others were angry.
A few stayed.

I turned my back on
the people who stayed.
I focused on my dent.
Well, it wasn't a dent
anymore but a small pit.
My Pit.

7

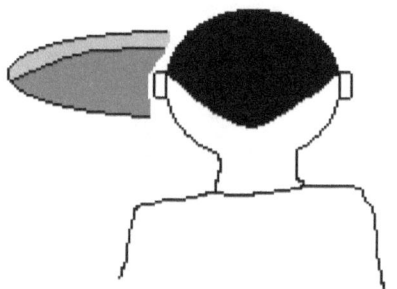

**I looked at the crowd and saw that
there were more people again.
All staring at the pit.
My Pit.**

8

I grew angrier. "Get Out!"
I screamed at them.
Once again they started to leave,
but a few still stayed.
My Pit grew bigger.

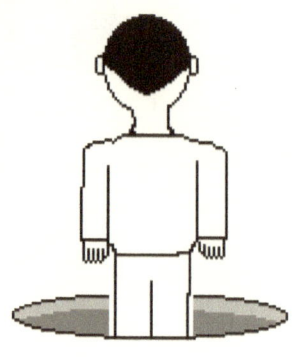

It was My Pit! I jumped in.
It was deeper
than I thought.
I still saw people looking
at me and My Pit.
It grew bigger.

I ignored the people who
were still watching.
It's My Pit and it
was becoming comfortable.
The pit grew bigger.

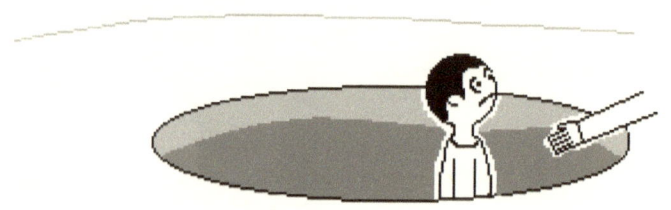

Soon the top was even with my waist.
I stood still in My Pit.
Someone then offered a hand.
I refused. My Pit grew bigger.

Someone offered another hand.
" Leave me alone!"
I raged at them.
My Pit grew bigger.

Soon I couldn't see anyone.
They were beyond the edges of My Pit.
The top was over my head.
I could still reach out
above the pit, but
I didn't want to.
My Pit grew bigger.

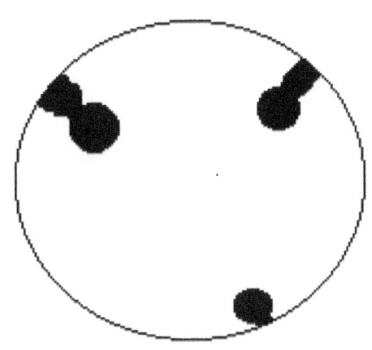

I became sad in the pit.
My Pit.
Occasionally I saw heads peek
over the edge but I ignored them.
What did they know?
The pit, My Pit, was comfortable
in an odd sort of way.

**Time went by and I paced back
and forth in the pit, My Pit.
It had grown so much bigger.
No more heads peeked over the edge.
I wondered why.**

16

As I paced I noticed a
small hole in the
bottom of My Pit.
It was so small I could
barely put a finger in it.
It was cold.

17

How could My Pit have a hole?
The small hole grew
a little bigger.
I looked into it.
I could not see anything.
I stuck my hand into it.
I could not feel anything.
It was very cold.

Once in a while I could hear faint voices
at the top of My Pit.
They were talking about me.
I couldn't understand them.
I looked up so seldom
that I didn't care about them anymore.
I focused on My Pit.

As My Pit grew,
so did the little hole.
It was still cold. I was cold.
I couldn't feel anything
except the bitter cold.

My Pit grew still bigger.
The small hole grew bigger.
It didn't have a bottom.
Or sides. Or anything but a rim.
Where did it go I wondered?
I wanted to find out.

21

I took a last look up.
The edge of My Pit
was way beyond my reach.
I couldn't get out even
if I wanted to. I didn't want to.
I looked at the
small hole again.
It was almost inviting.

The closer I looked at the small hole,
the bigger it became.
Almost inviting me to jump in.

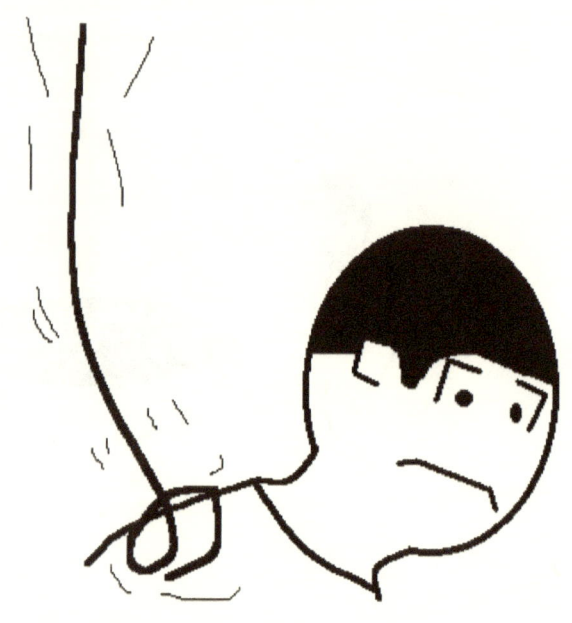

As I pondered the small hole,
something hit me on the back.
I looked up at a rope
that went up My Pit
and over the top.

**Down the rope came a person.
She was smiling.
I became angrier.
How dare she smile at me!**

25

I retreated to the other
side of the pit,
My Pit. She started to follow.
I turned my back to her.
After all this was My Pit.

She tried to talk me into climbing out of
My Pit. "NO WAY!" I cried.
She looked at the small hole.
She looked at me.

"WHAT?" I shouted.
"Going to jump?" she asked.
I looked at the small hole,
Long and hard.
"Maybe.",
I replied quietly.

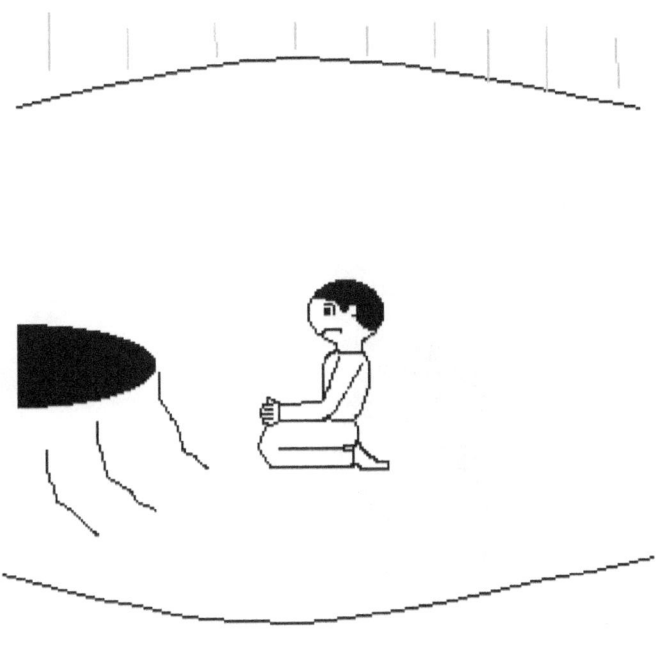

I sat down again and
continued to stare
at the small hole.
It continued to beckon.
What lay within?

I looked at her.
She looked at me.
She gestured at the rope.
I shook my head.
Saddened, she turned to leave.

30

I watched the rope jerk as
she climbed out of My Pit.
"About time." I thought.
But there was a sense of loss
and loneliness.
But I still had the pit, My Pit.

**Looking up I saw the edge
of My Pit far, far above me.
There was just a
glimmer of light at the top.**

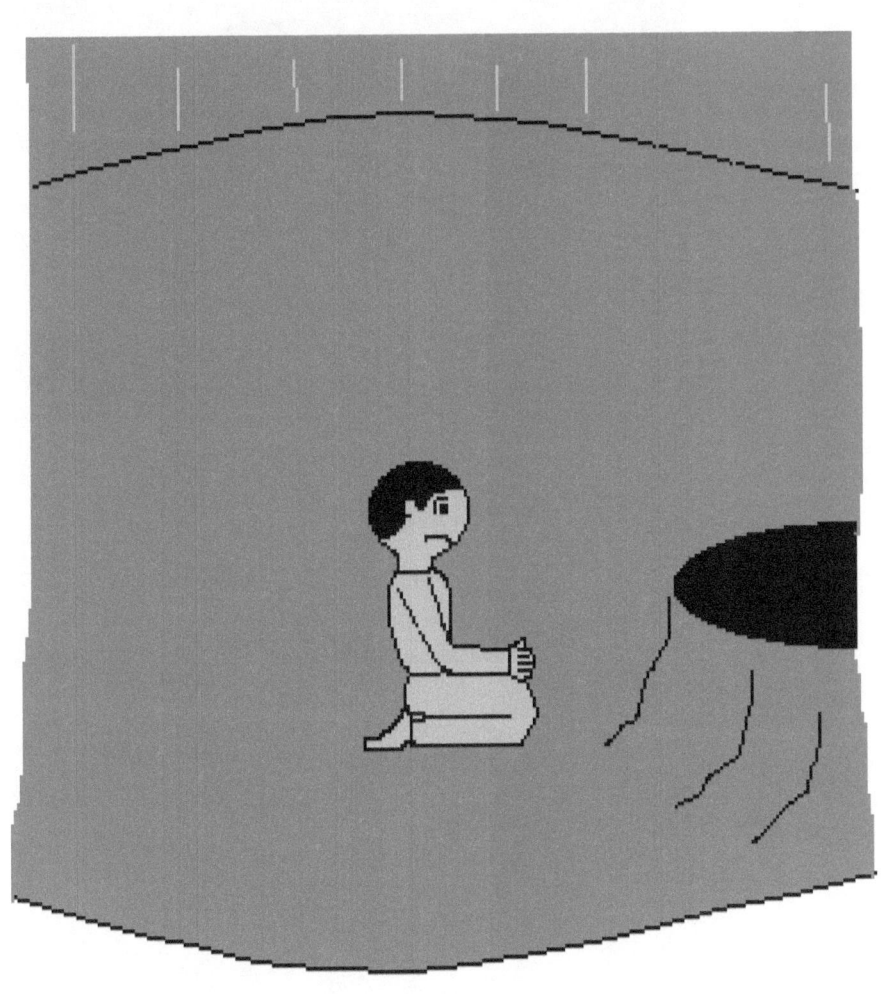

**Time passed as I sat there
at the bottom of My Pit.
It was dark here.
I hadn't noticed that before.
The small hole waited patiently.**

Finally I decided, I was going
to jump into the hole.
I felt better all of the sudden.
A sense of euphoria
and peace came over me.

I readied myself to jump
into the small hole.
I looked into its nothingness.
I flexed my knees. I jumped.

As I began to fall into
the small hole,
it seemed to lunge at me,
as if eager to engulf me.
I screamed and twisted
away from it.

36

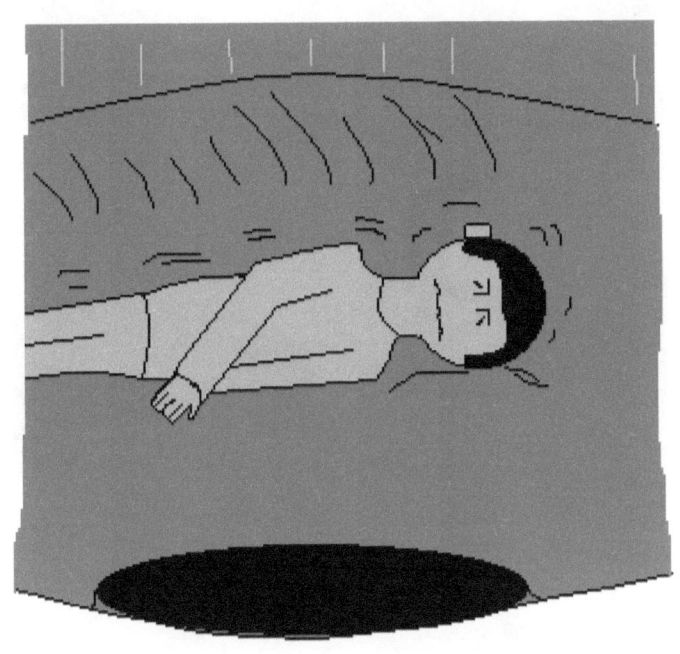

I hit the ground and lay there panting.
A minute ago I had been ready,
now I was frightened. Why?
Then I remembered the
girl who had wanted to help me.

I began to think.
Perhaps the pit, My Pit,
wasn't mine after all.
Maybe it was something else.
Maybe it wasn't as
comfortable as I thought.
I noticed the small hole
creeping towards me.

I scrambled to get out of its way.
I lunged for the rope,
missed and fell.
The ground around me
began to cave in.
The small hole was growing
bigger and bigger.

It was then that I prayed
and screamed for help.
I again reached for the rope.
The ground gave way,
I leaped. I held onto the
rope with all my might
over the void below me.
The pit, My Pit had become
the small hole, only it wasn't
so small after all.

The pit, My Pit, the small hole,
they were all the same now.
One infinite void waiting for me,
my very essence,
everything I was,
and wasn't.

41

My hands started to slip.
I again screamed for help.
I could not hear anything
but the squeak of my hand
on the rope and the deafening
silence of the void below.

How long I hung there
I'll never know.
It was an endless time
of intensive thought.
Would the people above
miss me?
I thought they wouldn't.
Would I miss me? I wasn't sure.

Now I wasn't so sure.
My hands slipped again.
I looked down.
How easy it would be to just
let go and have oblivion take me.
How hard it would be to climb up the rope.

Yet I had screamed for help.
Why had I done that?
Fear of the unknown?
Afraid to let go?
Or just reflex for survival?

The void was still waiting.
<Let go>, **it seemed to say**
in a deep soothing voice.
<Just let go and all will be well.>

My hands slipped yet again.
I was getting tired of hanging on.
The void tried
to comfort me.
<I offer an end to
weariness and worry.>
It was tempting. My fear was fading.
The void started to smile at me
as if it were my best friend.

"Hey!", a voice cried
down to me.
"You are not alone!
We care about you!"
Instantly the smile on
the void grew dark and vicious.
<HE IS MINE!> It screamed.

I looked up at a head peering over
the edge of My Pit.
It was the same person from earlier.
"Hold on just a little longer!"
she yelled.
Then she disappeared.

I was very afraid now.
The void was boiling
in rage trying to drag
me down into itself.
I looked into it and
saw its true nature.
It only offered pain, to me
and to the others above.

"YOU WILL NOT GET ME!"
I thundered into the void.
I then realized that
I could not stay in
this pit, it wasn't mine.
It belonged to no
one but itself.
It only offered false peace.

51

My grip slipped one last time,
then I started pulling myself
up the rope. I didn't get too far.
I was too tired, too weary, and too alone. The voi
would win. It started to laugh.
I wept. I tried to climb again but
I couldn't go any higher.
The laughter grew louder.

Just when all seemed lost,
when the laughter was
the loudest, I slipped and fell.
Something fell past me.
The laughter stopped abruptly,
followed by a
<NOOOOOOO!>

I landed on a clump of dirt.
It covered part of the void.
There was another thump.
More clumps were falling.
They were covering the void.

The void's scream became fainter
as the dirt continued to fall.
I looked up and saw several
heads looking over the edge of the pit.
They were saving me.
I used the rope to stay
above the flood
of dirt raining down.

The pit grew smaller and smaller.
I could hear the people above
cheering me on. More heads
looked down at me encouraging me
to come out. It took a long time
for them to fill the pit in,
but fill it they did.
I was eager to leave this pit.

The rope helped steady me and guided
me up the pit. Finally it was filled so that my head
just peered over the rim.
There were lots of people watching me
and cheering for me. They also
had stopped filling the pit.

I panicked! Why had they stopped?
Then I realized that now
I had to help myself out of
this pit. I carefully used
the rope to pull myself
the rest of the way out.

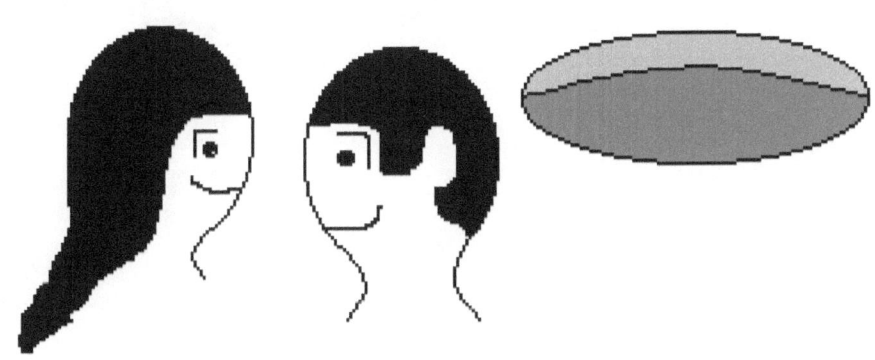

As I blinked at the light and
found my footing,
I was hugged by all
the people around me. It felt
good to be cared about and out of that pit,
My Former Pit. She was there smiling at me.
She gave me the biggest hug of all.
"Thanks." I said quietly.

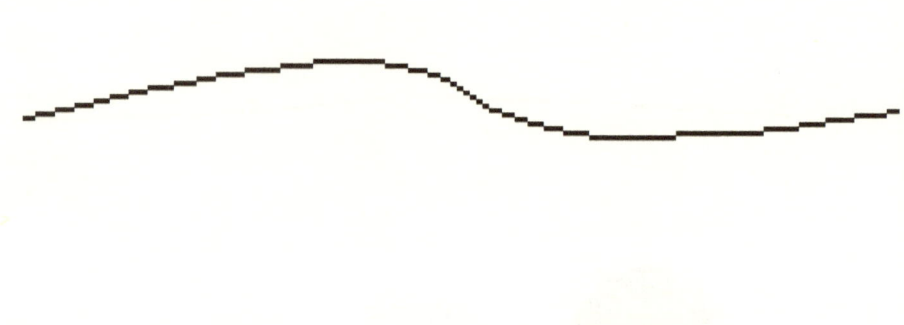

Today the pit is just a dent again.
I keep trying
to fill that last little bit
but I can't seem to get
rid of that dent.
I guess that dent is mine.
It serves as a reminder.